The Juicing Recipe Book

The Complete Guide to Making Homemade Fresh Juices

365 Days of Healthy and Delicious Recipes to Lose Weight, Detox Your Body and Live A Long Healthy Life

Doalt Hack

© Copyright 2022 By Doalt Hack

All Rights Reserved. No part of this publication or the information in it may be quoted from or reproduced in any form by means such as printing, scanning, photocopying or otherwise without prior written permission of the copyright holder.

CONTENT

INTRODUCTION 6
PRO TIPS FOR JUICING 7
HOW TO STORE EXTRA JUICE 8
JUICING AND WEIGHT LOSS 9

FRUIT-BASED JUICES 10
    Easy Apple Celery Juice 11
    Blueberry Beet Juice 12
    Morning Melon Boost 13
    Tutti-Frutti Juice 14
    Strawberry Lemonade Juice 15
    Berry Mint Blast 16
    Sparkling Kiwi Pineapple Juice 17
    Mango Melon Juice 18
    Cilantro Strawberry Banana Juice 19
    Blackberry Kiwi Juice Blend 20
    Pineapple Lavender Juice 21
    Honeydew Apple Juice 22
    Orange-Carrot Ginger Juice 23
    Sparkling Raspberry Pomegranate Juice 24
    Pretty in Pink Juice Blend 25
    Fruity Green Juice 26
    Papaya Pineapple Juice Blend 27
    Cucumber Melon Juice 28
    Mango Watermelon Juice 29
    Citrus Sunrise Juice 30
    Blueberry Beauty Juice 31
    Kiwi Orange Juice 32
    Peachy Pineapple Cooler 33
    Watermelon Gazpacho Juice 34
    Tropical Fruit Juice Blend 35
    Melon Agua Fresca 36
    Coconut Cabana Juice 37
    Razzle Dazzle Berry Juice 38
    Purple Peach Parsley Juice 39
    Jicama Pear Juice 40

Easy Breezy Citrus Blend 41
Apple Orchard Juice Blend 42
Raspberry Renewal Juice 43
Pink Grapefruit Delight 44
Blood Orange Bounty 45
Pear-fectly Delicious Juice 46
Black Cherry Almond Juice 47
Immunity-Boosting Blast 48
Banana Blackberry Juice 49
Pomegranate Peach Detox Blend 50
Passion Fruit Cocktail 51
Lemme at 'Em Juice 52
Grape Apple Punch 53

VEGETABLE-BASED JUICES 54
Ginger Beet Juice 55
Pick-Me-Up Juice Blend 56
Sweet Potato Power Juice 57
Calming Carrot Juice 58
Spicy Tomato Juice 59
Cucumber Celery Juice 60
Red Cabbage Carrot Juice 61
Ginger Green Juice Blend 62
Rockin' Radish Juice 63
Green Machine Juice Blend 64
Parsley Power Gulp 65
Tomato Gazpacho Juice 66
Spinach Lime Juice 67
Fabulous Fennel Juice Blend 68
Spirulina Avocado Juice 69
Refreshing Red Bell Pepper Carrot Juice 70
Skinny Green Juice 71
Carrot Celery Cleanse 72
Kick-Start Veggie Juice 73
Protein Power Juice 74
Breakfast of Champions Juice 75
Green Garden Delight 76
Cucumber Wake-Up Call 77
Best Foot Forward Juice 78

- Pumpkin Pie Juice 79
- Liver Detox Tonic 80
- Summer Squash Supreme 81
- Beet Berry Blast 82
- Minty Mojito Juice 83
- Cool Cilantro Coconut Juice 84

GREEN JUICES 85
- Beautiful Beet Juice 86
- Green Good Morning Juice 87
- Green Goodness Juice 88
- Glorious Green Juice 89
- Seven-Layer Green Juice 90
- Dreamy Green Juice 91
- Brilliant Brussels Juice 92
- Spicy Green Juice 93
- Mango Tango Green Juice 94
- Easy Peasy Green Lemonade 95
- Double Trouble Broccoli Juice 96
- Tossed Salad Juice 97
- Cool Cauliflower Juice 98
- Merry Melon Dream Juice 99
- Sensibly Sweet Juice 100
- Refreshing Green Juice 101
- Deeply Green Juice 102
- Beets Me Blend 103
- Simply Sweet Green Juice 104
- Rocket Fuel Green Juice 105
- Get-Up-and-Go Juice 106
- Sweet and Simple Green Juice 107
- Jolly Green Giant Juice 108
- Lean, Mean Green Juice 109
- Green Goddess Juice 110

CONCLUSION 111

INTRODUCTION

You may be tempted to think that juicing is just another health and fitness trend, or some kind of fad diet. In reality, however, it is a method through which you can easily increase your daily intake of essential nutrients while also cleansing your body and boosting your weight-loss efforts. If you have ever struggled to lose weight, juicing may be the solution you've been looking for.

You don't need to follow a diet plan prescribed by some health-and-fitness guru to successfully incorporate juicing into your diet. Juicing is easy and there is no wrong way to go about it. Create your own flavor combinations using your favorite fruits and vegetables, and throw in some healthy additives to boost the nutritional value of your juices. Once you start juicing, you may find yourself wondering why you waited so long to begin.

PRO TIPS FOR JUICING

To Remove Toxins, Soak Produce in Water with Vinegar

Your produce can pick up all sorts of harmful microorganisms on its way to your home. The acid in vinegar effectively kill some of those microorganisms. It needs to be in the correct ratio of water to vinegar. You want to use 3 parts water to 1-part vinegar. You can also buy commercial strength vinegar solutions that are more effective. If you're soaking your produce in the sink, make sure to clean your sink thoroughly first.

Juice Entire Fruit if Skin is Edible

You may not realize it, but you're losing a lot of nutrients when you peel many of your produce items. Half of the nutrition in an apple is held in its skins. Leaving edible skin will give you a huge amount of nutrients without affecting the flavor.

Remove Large Pits and Seeds Before Juicing

Always remove the hard seeds, stones, and pits from produce like apples, apricots, peaches, etc. They're not easy for the juicer to break down and will cause your juice to breakdown over time. Many of them also contain small amounts of cyanide which can be harmful to your health in large doses.

Stringy Vegetables Are Difficult to Juice

For stringy vegetables like spinach and celery may clog up your juicer. You can help with this problem by alternating your stringy vegetables with a hard vegetable like a carrot. Pre-cutting your strain vegetables to a quarter inch long also helps. Always clean your juicer after using it to help keep clogs from forming.

HOW TO STORE EXTRA JUICE

Store Leftover Juice in a Glass Container with an Airtight Lid

Glass containers are the best way to store extra juice. You can purchase Mason jars in several sizes which are perfect for various juice needs. Using small (half-jars) are great for taking an extra serving with you in the car. Larger sizes are perfect for juice for the family. The lids are interchangeable.

Fill Containers All the Way to the Top to Keep Air from Reducing Lifespan.

You want to avoid allowing air into the jar, so fill the jar to the top and tightly secure the lid. Adding a few drops of lemon juice will keep the juice fresh longer.

Freeze Juice in Freezer Bags or Ice Trays for Easier Access

Again, air is the enemy. Use various sizes of freezer zipper bags to freeze juices. Use a sharpie to label and date the juice. Freeze in ice trays for fun treats for the children. Adding a popsicle stick makes these juice cubes perfect for a summer treat. Use juice cubes in a different flavor juice for fun and creative flavors. CHAPTER SIX

JUICING AND WEIGHT LOSS

How Juicing Promotes Weight Loss

There are many reasons why juicing is helpful in promoting weight loss. For one thing, replacing typical meals of processed or fast foods with freshly squeezed juice will not only provide an increase in nutrient content, but it will also offer a significant reduction in calories. The basic science of weight loss is this: if you burn more calories than you consume, you will lose weight. This doesn't mean that you have to spend two hours on the treadmill every day just to burn off the food you eat. Remember that your body burns calories throughout the day just by keeping your heart pumping and your other organs functioning.

Unfortunately, many individuals in Western culture take in way too many calories on a daily basis: much more than their bodies need to function. This results in excess calories that are not immediately needed being converted to fat and stored. If a majority of those excess calories are derived from processed or fast foods, the toxins from those foods will also be stored along with the new fat cells. Over time, your body becomes literally weighed down, and your organs may not function as well as they once did. This can lead to more weight gain, making it a self-perpetuating cycle.

The key to losing weight is to create a calorie deficit so your body has to burn stored fat for fuel. Do not misconstrue this to mean that you should only consume a few hundred calories a day—you may lose weight quickly using this method, but it will be neither healthy nor sustainable. Your body needs a certain number of calories each day just to function, and if you go below that number, it could have negative effects on your health and even halt your weight loss entirely. The minimum number of calories your body requires on a daily basis to maintain necessary functions is referred to as your basal metabolic rate (BMR).

As part of a healthy diet, juicing may help you lose weight by encouraging the flushing of excess toxins from your body, by increasing your nutrient intake, and by helping you create a calorie deficit. When you replace unhealthy, toxin-laden foods with nutrient-packed juices, you can start to restore the healthy function of your organs. Once your body is no longer being overloaded with incoming toxins, it can begin to rid itself of stored toxins. All of the nutrients in freshly pressed juices will boost your immune system and improve your organ function and overall health.

Another significant benefit of juicing for weight loss is that fruits and vegetables act as natural appetite suppressants. If you have heard about the nasty side effects associated with commercial appetite suppressants, or if you have tried them yourself, you should be thrilled to learn that the solution is much easier than you may have thought. Because fruits and vegetables are so high in dietary fiber and other nutrients, they will help to decrease your appetite and curb cravings. If you don't have to fight feeling hungry all day, you are more likely to stick to your diet plan and achieve the weight loss you desire!

FRUIT-BASED JUICES

"Fruit juices are a smart addition to any well-balanced diet, providing vitamins and minerals like potassium, vitamin C, and folate. Fruit juice is also a convenient way for adults and children to help reach the recommended number of daily servings of fruit and vegetables. Just one 4-ounce glass of 100-percent juice provides a full serving of fruit."

Easy Apple Celery Juice
SERVES 2

As simple as it is, this juice is surprisingly tasty. The combination of crisp apples and celery with a splash of lime juice is refreshing, rejuvenating, and incredibly good for you!

3 Medium Apples
2 Medium Stalks Celery
2 Tablespoons Freshly Squeezed Lime Juice

1. Peel, cut, deseed, and/or chop the ingredients as needed.

2. Place a container under the juicer's spout.

3. Feed the apples and celery through the juicer.

4. Stir the lime juice into the juice and pour into glasses to serve.

Blueberry Beet Juice
SERVES 2

Blueberries contain flavonoids, a powerful antioxidant, as well as a type of dietary fiber called pectin. In combination with the vitamin and mineral content of beets, this juice packs a powerful nutritional punch.

2 Cups Blueberries
2 Small Beets
1 Small Apple

1. Peel, cut, deseed, and/or chop the ingredients as needed.

2. Place a container under the juicer's spout.

3. Feed the ingredients one at a time, in the order listed, through the juicer.

4. Stir the juice and pour into glasses to serve.

Morning Melon Boost

SERVES 2

Melons such as watermelon and honeydew are an excellent source of adenosine, a chemical that helps reduce risk of stroke and cancer. Combined with the cool flavor of cantaloupe and the tang of lemon, this juice will definitely wake you up.

2 Cups Watermelon
2 Cups Cantaloupe
2 Cups Honeydew
½ Lemon

1. Peel, cut, deseed, and/or chop the ingredients as needed.

2. Place a container under the juicer's spout.

3. Feed the ingredients one at a time, in the order listed, through the juicer.

4. Stir the juice and pour into glasses to serve.

Tutti-Frutti Juice
SERVES 2

This juice is a refreshing blend of fresh fruit, sure to tickle your taste buds. In addition to its delicious flavor, this juice is full of powerful antioxidants that will help repair cellular damage caused by free radicals.

1 Ripe Grapefruit
1 Cup Blueberries
1 Cup Red Grapes
1 Small Apple

1. Peel, cut, deseed, and/or chop the ingredients as needed.

2. Place a container under the juicer's spout.

3. Feed the ingredients one at a time, in the order listed, through the juicer.

4. Stir the juice and pour into glasses to serve.

Strawberry Lemonade Juice

SERVES 4

Juicing doesn't have to involve gulping down glasses of green liquid all day—it can be as cool and refreshing as this strawberry lemonade juice. Share it with family and friends, or keep it to yourself for a lazy day lounging by the pool.

1 Cup Strawberries
3 Lemons
3 Cups Cold Water
1 Tablespoon Raw Honey (Optional)

1. Peel, cut, deseed, and/or chop the ingredients as needed.

2. Place a container under the juicer's spout.

3. Feed the strawberries and lemons through the juicer.

4. Stir the water and honey into the juice and pour into glasses to serve.

Berry Mint Blast

SERVES 2

Fresh mint helps reduce both inflammation and indigestion, and it also contains omega-3 fatty acids, which support healthy hair and skin growth. Combining mint with the fresh flavor of mixed berries makes for a juice that will leave you wanting more.

2 Cups Blueberries
1 Cup Strawberries
1 Cup Raspberries
½ Cup Currants (Optional)
1 Bunch Mint Leaves

1. Peel, cut, deseed, and/or chop the ingredients as needed.

2. Place a container under the juicer's spout.

3. Feed the ingredients one at a time, in the order listed, through the juicer.

4. Stir the juice and pour into glasses to serve.

Sparkling Kiwi Pineapple Juice

SERVES 2

No one said that fresh-pressed juice had to be boring. This fizzy fruit juice is full of healthy nutrients, and the addition of sparkling water gives it a little bit of extra class.

1 Small Pineapple
3 Ripe Kiwis
1 Cup Sparkling Water

1. Peel, cut, deseed, and/or chop the ingredients as needed.

2. Place a container under the juicer's spout.

3. Feed the pineapple and kiwis through the juicer.

4. Stir the sparkling water into the juice and pour into glasses to serve.

Mango Melon Juice
SERVES 2

The sweet combination of mangoes and melons is enough to make you crave this incredible juice. The fact that it is loaded with antioxidants and other nutrients is just a bonus!

2 Ripe Mangoes
2 Cups Watermelon
1 Cup Cantaloupe
1 Tablespoon Freshly Squeezed Lemon Juice

1. Peel, cut, deseed, and/or chop the ingredients as needed.

2. Place a container under the juicer's spout.

3. Feed the mangoes, watermelon, and cantaloupe through the juicer.

4. Stir the lemon juice into the juice and pour into glasses to serve.

Cilantro Strawberry Banana Juice
SERVES 2

There is nothing quite like the taste of fresh cilantro to liven things up. Not only is this herb full of spicy flavor, it's also loaded with phyto-nutrients that help lower bad cholesterol and raise good cholesterol.

2 Cups Strawberries
1 Cup Cilantro
1 Cup Cold Water
1 Small Banana

1. Peel, cut, deseed, and/or chop the ingredients as needed.

2. Place a container under the juicer's spout.

3. Feed the strawberries and cilantro through the juicer.

4. In a blender, combine the water and banana and blend until smooth.

5. Add the strawberry cilantro juice and pulse to blend.

6. Pour into glasses and serve.

Blackberry Kiwi Juice Blend
SERVES 2

Kiwi is rich in vitamin C, which is essential for healing wounds and keeping teeth and gums healthy. Combined with the antioxidant power of blackberries, this juice blend is both good and good for you!

2 Cups Blackberries
2 Ripe Kiwis
1 Medium Apple
6 Sprigs Cilantro

1. Peel, cut, deseed, and/or chop the ingredients as needed.

2. Place a container under the juicer's spout.

3. Feed the ingredients one at a time, in the order listed, through the juicer.

4. Stir the juice and pour into glasses to serve.

Pineapple Lavender Juice
SERVES 1

If you are looking for a unique and refreshing beverage to serve at a luncheon, or just something sweet to enjoy by yourself, this pineapple lavender juice is sure to please.

1 Pineapple
1 Tablespoon Lavender Blossoms

1. Peel, cut, deseed, and/or chop the ingredients as needed.

2. Place a container under the juicer's spout.

3. Feed the pineapple through the juicer.

4. Using a mortar and pestle, grind the lavender blossoms into a powder.

5. Stir the lavender powder into the pineapple juice and pour into a glass to serve.

Honeydew Apple Juice
SERVES 2

If you aren't a fan of overly sweet juices, this one is just right for you. The mildness of honeydew combined with the slightly sweet flavor of apple is perfectly balanced with the crisp, refreshing kale in this juice.

2 Medium Apples
1 Small Honeydew
4 Small Kale Leaves

1. Peel, cut, deseed, and/or chop the ingredients as needed.

2. Place a container under the juicer's spout.

3. Feed the ingredients one at a time, in the order listed, through the juicer.

4. Stir the juice and pour into glasses to serve.

Orange-Carrot Ginger Juice

SERVES 2

The fresh flavor of orange juice in this recipe is enough to mellow out the carrot and ginger. As a result, you get all the nutritional benefits of carrots and ginger while enjoying the classic orange juice tang!

4 Medium Carrots
2 Medium Navel Oranges
1 Small Apple
1-Inch Piece Gingerroot

1. Peel, cut, deseed, and/or chop the ingredients as needed.

2. Place a container under the juicer's spout.

3. Feed the ingredients one at a time, in the order listed, through the juicer.

4. Stir the juice and pour into glasses to serve.

Sparkling Raspberry Pomegranate Juice
SERVES 2

This sparkling juice is unique and satisfying. If you are looking for a new and interesting recipe to shake things up, look no further!

2 Cups Raspberries
2 Ripe Pomegranates
1 Cup Sparkling Water

1. Peel and remove the seeds from the pomegranate.

2. Place a container under the juicer's spout.

3. Feed the raspberries and pomegranate seeds through the juicer.

4. Stir the sparkling water into the juice and pour into glasses to serve.

Pretty in Pink Juice Blend
SERVES 2

This pretty pink juice is lightly sweet and full of fruit flavor. Although you may find it difficult to share, your family and friends are sure to enjoy this sweet beverage just as much as you will.

3 Cups Watermelon
2 Cups Raspberries
1 Cup Strawberries

1. Peel, cut, deseed, and/or chop the ingredients as needed.

2. Place a container under the juicer's spout.

3. Feed the ingredients one at a time, in the order listed, through the juicer.

4. Stir the juice and pour into glasses to serve.

Fruity Green Juice
SERVES 2

Drinking a glass of liquid spinach may not sound appealing to you, but a glass of apple-pear-orange juice might! Using fruit juices to disguise the flavor of vegetables is both simple and delicious.

1 Bunch Spinach Leaves
1 Medium Apple
1 Medium Pear
1 Medium Navel Orange

1. Peel, cut, deseed, and/or chop the ingredients as needed.

2. Place a container under the juicer's spout.

3. Feed the ingredients one at a time, in the order listed, through the juicer.

4. Stir the juice and pour into glasses to serve.

Papaya Pineapple Juice Blend
SERVES 2

Pineapple contains a number of anti-inflammatory compounds, and papayas contain enzymes to promote healthy digestion. All in all, this juice will have you feeling just like new.

1 Small Pineapple
1 Papaya
1 Small Apple

1. Peel, cut, deseed, and/or chop the ingredients as needed.

2. Place a container under the juicer's spout.

3. Feed the ingredients one at a time, in the order listed, through the juicer.

4. Stir the juice and pour into glasses to serve.

Cucumber Melon Juice
SERVES 2

When it comes to refreshment, nothing beats this cucumber melon juice. The flavors of watermelon, cantaloupe, and honeydew blend perfectly with the water content of cucumber to create a cool, delectable beverage.

2 Medium Cucumbers
1 Cup Watermelon
1 Cup Cantaloupe
1 Cup Honeydew

1. Peel, cut, deseed, and/or chop the ingredients as needed.

2. Place a container under the juicer's spout.

3. Feed the ingredients one at a time, in the order listed, through the juicer.

4. Stir the juice and pour into glasses to serve.

Mango Watermelon Juice

SERVES 2

The sweet, succulent flavor of mango blends perfectly with the mild sweetness of watermelon in this juice. In addition to its fresh fruit flavor, this juice is loaded with antioxidants.

3 Cups Watermelon
1 Ripe Mango
1 Tablespoon Freshly Squeezed Lemon Juice

1. Peel, cut, deseed, and/or chop the ingredients as needed.

2. Place a container under the juicer's spout.

3. Feed the watermelon and mango through the juicer.

4. Stir the lemon juice into the juice and pour into glasses to serve.

Citrus Sunrise Juice
SERVES 2

This juice is very easy to make—you don't even need a juicer! Simply juice the citrus fruits by hand and layer each juice in glasses to serve. This beverage is as beautiful as it is refreshing.

2 Medium Blood Oranges, Halved
2 Medium Navel Oranges, Halved
1 Small Pink Grapefruit, Halved

1. Using a citrus press or hand juicer, juice the blood oranges. Divide the juice between two glasses.

2. Juice the navel oranges and divide the juice between the glasses.

3. Juice the grapefruit, divide the juice between the glasses, and serve.

Blueberry Beauty Juice
SERVES 2

Blueberries are loaded with antioxidants. Combined with the fiber content of apples, this juice will help to flush toxins from your body, making your skin clear and your hair silky smooth.

1 ½ Cups Blueberries
1 Cup Pineapple
1 Medium Apple

1. Peel, cut, deseed, and/or chop the ingredients as needed.

2. Place a container under the juicer's spout.

3. Feed the ingredients one at a time, in the order listed, through the juicer.

4. Stir the juice and pour into glasses to serve.

Kiwi Orange Juice
SERVES 2

Oranges are known for their vitamin C content, but they also have been shown to help shrink tumors and reduce inflammation. Add the anti-aging properties of kiwi, and this juice is quite the nutritional wonder.

3 Medium Navel Oranges
3 Ripe Kiwis
1 Teaspoon Lime Zest

1. Peel, cut, deseed, and/or chop the ingredients as needed.

2. Place a container under the juicer's spout.

3. Feed the oranges and kiwis through the juicer.

4. Stir the lime zest into the juice and pour into glasses to serve.

Peachy Pineapple Cooler
SERVES 2

Whether you are in the mood for a sweet snack or are looking for a refreshing beverage to enjoy by the pool, this peachy pineapple cooler is the perfect drink.

2 Medium Peaches Or Nectarines
1 Small Pineapple
1 Small Apple
½ Cup Sparkling Water

1. Peel, cut, deseed, and/or chop the ingredients as needed.

2. Place a container under the juicer's spout.

3. Feed the peaches, pineapple, and apple through the juicer.

4. Stir the sparkling water into the juice and pour into glasses to serve.

Watermelon Gazpacho Juice
SERVES 2

Watermelon gazpacho is a cool summer soup made from watermelon and cucumber. This recipe combines all of the delicious and healthy ingredients of watermelon gazpacho into a sippable beverage.

3 Cups Watermelon
1 Cup Cucumber
1 Tablespoon Freshly Squeezed Lime Juice

1. Peel, cut, deseed, and/or chop the ingredients as needed.

2. Place a container under the juicer's spout.

3. Feed the watermelon and cucumber through the juicer.

4. Stir the lime juice into the juice and pour into glasses to serve.

Tropical Fruit Juice Blend
SERVES 2

Pineapple is an excellent source of vitamin C, iron, and potassium. It also contains bromelain and other anti-inflammatory compounds that help to promote joint health.

1 Ripe Mango
1 Medium Orange
½ Pineapple
1 Banana

1. Peel, cut, deseed, and/or chop the ingredients as needed.

2. Place a container under the juicer's spout.

3. Feed the mango, orange, and pineapple through the juicer.

4. In a blender, blend the banana until smooth.

5. Stir the pureed banana into the juice and pour into glasses to serve.

Melon Agua Fresca

SERVES 2

This cool, refreshing beverage simply can't be beat. Not only is it sure to satisfy your thirst, but the melons in this recipe will provide the added bonus of both anti-cancer and antioxidant properties.

½ Small Cantaloupe
½ Small Honeydew
½ Lime
1½ Cups Cold Water

1. Peel, cut, deseed, and/or chop the ingredients as needed.

2. Place a container under the juicer's spout.

3. Feed the cantaloupe, honeydew, and lime through the juicer.

4. Stir the water into the juice and pour into glasses to serve.

Coconut Cabana Juice

SERVES 2

Sweet and simple, this juice is just what you need to slake your thirst. Coconut water is rich in electrolytes and other ingredients that ensure proper hydration. Combined with the sweetness of pineapple and a hint of lime, this coconut cabana juice is perfect!

1 Cup Pineapple
½ Lime
2 Cups Coconut Water

1. Peel, cut, deseed, and/or chop the ingredients as needed.

2. Place a container under the juicer's spout.

3. Feed the pineapple and lime through the juicer.

4. Stir the coconut water into the juice and pour into glasses to serve.

Razzle Dazzle Berry Juice
SERVES 2

Strawberries are known to have antiviral, anti-cancer, and antioxidant properties. Factor in their vitamin C content, and that makes these berries an incredibly healthy ingredient well suited to this dazzling berry juice.

2 Cups Blackberries Or Raspberries
1 Cup Blueberries
1 Cup Strawberries
½ Cup Cold Water
1 Tablespoon Orange Zest

1. Place a container under the juicer's spout.

2. Feed the berries through the juicer.

3. Stir the water and orange zest into the juice and pour into glasses to serve.

Purple Peach Parsley Juice
SERVES 2

This refreshing juice blend is just what you need to cool down on a hot day. It also makes a wonderful breakfast drink—sure to keep you fueled and focused throughout the morning.

2 Medium Peaches
1 Medium Apple
1 Cup Blueberries
1 Cup Parsley Leaves

1. Peel, cut, deseed, and/or chop the ingredients as needed.

2. Place a container under the juicer's spout.

3. Feed the ingredients one at a time, in the order listed, through the juicer.

4. Stir the juice and pour into glasses to serve.

Jicama Pear Juice

SERVES 2

Jicama is a type of root vegetable known for its fiber content. In combination with carrots, pear, and lemon, this wonderful ingredient makes a fortifying juice.

2 Cups Jicama
2 Medium Carrots
1 Medium Pear
½ Lemon
½ Lime

1. Peel, cut, deseed, and/or chop the ingredients as needed.

2. Place a container under the juicer's spout.

3. Feed the ingredients one at a time, in the order listed, through the juicer.

4. Stir the juice and pour into glasses to serve.

Easy Breezy Citrus Blend
SERVES 2

Citrus fruits are an excellent source of healthy vitamins and minerals. This recipe is the perfect combination of tangerine, orange, and grapefruit juice flavored with a hint of lime.

2 Medium Tangerines
1 Medium Navel Orange
½ Small Pink Grapefruit
½ Lime
1 Cup Cold Water

1. Peel, cut, deseed, and/or chop the ingredients as needed.

2. Place a container under the juicer's spout.

3. Feed the citrus fruits through the juicer.

4. Stir the water into the juice and pour into glasses to serve.

Apple Orchard Juice Blend
SERVES 2

There are so many different varieties of apple that it can be difficult to choose just one. But who says you have to? This recipe utilizes four different types of apple to produce a crisp and delicious juice blend.

2 Medium Golden Delicious Apples
1 Medium Granny Smith Apple
1 Medium Gala Apple
1 Medium Red Delicious Apple

1. Peel, cut, deseed, and/or chop the ingredients as needed.

2. Place a container under the juicer's spout.

3. Feed the apples through the juicer.

4. Stir the juice and pour into glasses to serve.

Raspberry Renewal Juice
SERVES 2

Like all berries, raspberries contain vitamins C, K, and E. In addition, raspberries are a good source of folate, copper, iron, and manganese. They have also been linked to reduced cholesterol and have been shown to inhibit the growth of certain types of cancer.

2 Cups Raspberries
1 Large Carrot
1 Medium Pear
1 Tablespoon Freshly Squeezed Lemon Juice

1. Peel, cut, deseed, and/or chop the ingredients as needed.

2. Place a container under the juicer's spout.

3. Feed the raspberries, carrot, and pear through the juicer.

4. Stir the lemon juice into the juice and pour into glasses to serve.

Pink Grapefruit Delight
SERVES 2

Grapefruit is rich in vitamin C like all citrus fruits, but that's not all it's good for. This fruit also contains limonene, a compound that has been shown to reduce the risk for breast cancer.

2 Small Pink Grapefruits
2 Limes
1 Cup Cold Water
1 Tablespoon Raw Honey (Optional)
1 Teaspoon Lemon Zest

1. Peel, cut, deseed, and/or chop the ingredients as needed.

2. Place a container under the juicer's spout.

3. Feed the grapefruits and limes through the juicer.

4. Stir the water, honey, and lemon zest into the juice and pour into glasses to serve.

Blood Orange Bounty
SERVES 2

Blood oranges differ from traditional navel oranges in more than just color. The dark red pigment that gives the blood orange its name is the result of high levels of anthocyanins—these pigments act as an antioxidant, which makes blood oranges a better source than their orange sisters.

3 Large Blood Oranges
2 Medium Apples
1 Large Carrot
1 Large Stalk Celery

1. Peel, cut, deseed, and/or chop the ingredients as needed.

2. Place a container under the juicer's spout.

3. Feed the ingredients one at a time, in the order listed, through the juicer.

4. Stir the juice and pour into glasses to serve.

Pear-fectly Delicious Juice
SERVES 2

Pears have been used as a natural diuretic and digestive aid for centuries. Combining them with the cool flavor and high-water content of cucumber in this recipe makes for a very refreshing beverage.

2 Medium Pears
1 Small Cucumber
1 Sprig Mint

1. Peel, cut, deseed, and/or chop the ingredients as needed.

2. Place a container under the juicer's spout.

3. Feed the ingredients one at a time, in the order listed, through the juicer.

4. Stir the juice and pour into glasses to serve.

Black Cherry Almond Juice
SERVES 2

Black cherries are a good source of iron, which is essential for producing healthy blood cells. In addition, they also contain ellagic acid, a compound that has anti-cancer properties.

2 Cups Black Cherries
2 Cups Cold Water
¼ Cup Raw Almonds

1. Peel, cut, deseed, and/or chop the ingredients as needed.

2. Place a container under the juicer's spout.

3. Feed the cherries through the juicer.

4. In a blender, combine the cherry juice, water, and almonds and blend until smooth.

5. Pour into glasses and serve.

Immunity-Boosting Blast
SERVES 2

The fruits and cilantro in this juice are full of immunity-boosting power. Packed with vitamin C, calcium, and other nutrients, these ingredients are sure to make you feel healthier and more alive.

2 Medium Navel Oranges
2 Ripe Kiwis
1 Small Pink Grapefruit
1 Lemon
6 Sprigs Cilantro

1. Peel, cut, deseed, and/or chop the ingredients as needed.

2. Place a container under the juicer's spout.

3. Feed the ingredients one at a time, in the order listed, through the juicer.

4. Stir the juice and pour into glasses to serve.

Banana Blackberry Juice

SERVES 2

Bananas are an excellent source of vitamin C, magnesium, and potassium, all of which help to replenish your body's stores of electrolytes. With the refreshing flavor of blackberries, this juice is the perfect post-workout drink.

    2 Cups Blackberries
    1 Medium Apple
    1 Small Banana

1. Peel, cut, deseed, and/or chop the ingredients as needed.

2. Place a container under the juicer's spout.

3. Feed the blackberries and apple through the juicer.

4. In a blender, blend the banana until smooth.

5. Stir the pureed banana into the juice and pour into glasses to serve.

Pomegranate Peach Detox Blend
SERVES 2

Peaches are more than just a sweet, scrumptious fruit—they are also a good source of niacin (B3), which has been shown to reduce the risk for cardiovascular disease.

2 Pomegranates
2 Medium Peaches
1 Medium Navel Orange
1 Medium Apple

1. Peel, cut, deseed, and/or chop the ingredients as needed. Remove and save the seeds from the pomegranate, while discarding the rest of the fruit.

2. Place a container under the juicer's spout.

3. Feed the ingredients one at a time, in the order listed, through the juicer.

4. Stir the juice and pour into glasses to serve.

Passion Fruit Cocktail

SERVES 2

If you've never had passion fruit juice before, you don't know what you're missing. Not only do these fruits produce delicious juice, but they're also loaded with dietary fiber, vitamin A, and beta-carotene. This is a hand-pressed juice that doesn't require a juicer.

3 Medium Passion Fruit, Halved
1 Medium Navel Orange, Halved
1 Cup Cold Water
1 Teaspoon Orange Zest

1. Using a hand juicer, juice the passion fruit and pour the juice in a container.

2. Juice the orange by hand and add the juice to the container.

3. Stir the water and orange zest into the juice and pour into glasses to serve.

Lemme at 'Em Juice
SERVES 2

Lemons have been labeled as one of the most powerful fruits for detoxification—they have also been linked to cancer prevention and reduced risk for heart disease and stroke. Combining them with a variety of other nutritious ingredients makes this recipe an excellent addition to your juicing regimen.

1 Romaine Lettuce Heart
2 Medium Green Apples
2 Medium Pears
1 Large Carrot
1 Large Stalk Celery
1 Lemon
1 Lime

1. Peel, cut, deseed, and/or chop the ingredients as needed.

2. Place a container under the juicer's spout.

3. Feed the ingredients one at a time, in the order listed, through the juicer.

4. Stir the juice and pour into glasses to serve.

Grape Apple Punch

SERVES 2

Grapes are an excellent source of vitamins A, B, and C; they are also rich in minerals, including calcium, iron, and selenium. The antioxidants in the fruit have also been shown to have antiaging properties. This juice will do more than quench your thirst—it will kick your body into gear!

2 Cups Seedless Red Grapes
1 Medium Apple
1 Cup Kale Leaves
1 Cup Spinach
½ Cup Cold Water

1. Peel, cut, deseed, and/or chop the ingredients as needed.

2. Place a container under the juicer's spout.

3. Feed the grapes, apple, kale, and spinach through the juicer.

4. Stir the water into the juice and pour into glasses to serve.

VEGETABLE-BASED JUICES

"One of the benefits of vegetables is that they have low energy density, meaning that you can eat a lot of vegetables without eating a lot of calories. This has powerful implications when it comes to weight loss—eating fewer calories while still feeling full and satisfied."

Ginger Beet Juice
SERVES 2

To make this refreshing juice, you don't even need a juicer. All you have to do is combine the ingredients in your blender and add enough water to reach the desired consistency.

2 Medium Beets
2 Large Carrots
1 Medium Apple
1 Cup Cold Water
1-Inch Piece Gingerroot

1. In a blender, combine all of the ingredients and blend until as smooth as possible.

2. Press the mixture through a fine mesh strainer until all of the juice is out.

3. Discard the pulp, pour into glasses, and serve.

Pick-Me-Up Juice Blend
SERVES 2

This juice blend is the perfect combination of leafy greens and bright fresh fruit. You get all of the nutritional benefits of kale, dandelion greens, and parsley, and the zesty flavor of green apple and lime.

1 Medium Green Apple
2 Large Kale Leaves
½ Bunch Dandelion Greens
½ Bunch Parsley Leaves
½ Lime

1. Peel, cut, deseed, and/or chop the ingredients as needed.

2. Place a container under the juicer's spout.

3. Feed the ingredients one at a time, in the order listed, through the juicer.

4. Stir the juice and pour into glasses to serve.

Sweet Potato Power Juice

SERVES 2

Sweet potatoes are known for their unique flavor and their benefits related to detoxification and digestive health. Sweet potatoes are also a good source of copper, iron, manganese, and magnesium.

2 Medium Apples
2 Small Beets
1 Large Sweet Potato
1 Large Carrot
1 Small Red Bell Pepper

1. Peel, cut, deseed, and/or chop the ingredients as needed.

2. Place a container under the juicer's spout.

3. Feed the ingredients one at a time, in the order listed, through the juicer.

4. Stir the juice and pour into glasses to serve.

Calming Carrot Juice
SERVES 2

This carrot juice is just what you need to help you relax after a long, stressful day. The vitamins and minerals in the ingredients will help your body to recharge and refuel.

6 Medium Carrots
2 Large Stalks Celery
1 Small Orange

1. Peel, cut, deseed, and/or chop the ingredients as needed.

2. Place a container under the juicer's spout.

3. Feed the ingredients one at a time, in the order listed, through the juicer.

4. Stir the juice and pour into glasses to serve.

Spicy Tomato Juice

SERVES 2

This spicy tomato juice may be just what you need to bring you out of a funk. Packed with nutrients and the kick of red chili, this is like nothing you've ever tried before.

6 Plum Tomatoes
1 Medium Red Bell Pepper
1 Large Carrot
1 Small Cucumber
1 Red Chili Pepper

1. Peel, cut, deseed, and/or chop the ingredients as needed.

2. Place a container under the juicer's spout.

3. Feed the ingredients one at a time, in the order listed, through the juicer.

4. Stir the juice and pour into glasses to serve.

Cucumber Celery Juice

SERVES 2

This recipe is perfect for a juice cleanse or detox because it is low in calories but high in water content. In addition, both cucumber and celery are good sources of healthy nutrients, which will boost the flushing of toxins from your body.

2 Large Stalks Celery
1 Small Head Broccoli
1 Cucumber
1 Small Pear
½ Bunch Parsley Leaves

1. Peel, cut, deseed, and/or chop the ingredients as needed.

2. Place a container under the juicer's spout.

3. Feed the ingredients one at a time, in the order listed, through the juicer.

4. Stir the juice and pour into glasses to serve.

Red Cabbage Carrot Juice

SERVES 2

Cabbage is one of very few vegetables that contain vitamin E. It's also a good source of sulfur, which helps to purify the blood and detoxify the liver.

4 Large Swiss Chard Leaves
2 Large Carrots
1 Medium Apple
¼ Small Head Red Cabbage
2 Tablespoons Freshly Squeezed Lemon Juice

1. Peel, cut, deseed, and/or chop the ingredients as needed.

2. Place a container under the juicer's spout.

3. Feed the Swiss chard, carrots, apple, and cabbage through the juicer.

4. Stir the lemon juice into the juice and pour into glasses to serve.

Ginger Green Juice Blend
SERVES 2

Flavored with ginger and sweetened with apple, this juice is something entirely unique and completely refreshing.

1 Cup Baby Spinach Leaves
1 Large Carrot
1 Large Stalk Celery
½ Bunch Kale Leaves
½ Small Cucumber
1 Medium Apple
1-Inch Piece Gingerroot

1. Peel, cut, deseed, and/or chop the ingredients as needed.

2. Place a container under the juicer's spout.

3. Feed the ingredients one at a time, in the order listed, through the juicer.

4. Stir the juice and pour into glasses to serve.

Rockin' Radish Juice

SERVES 2

Radishes are rich in vitamin C, folic acid, and anthocyanins, which make them valuable as a cancer-fighting food. The vegetables in this recipe also contain a combination of vitamins that help to treat skin disorders.

8 Small Radishes With Greens
2 Cups Baby Spinach Leaves
1 Large Carrot
1 Large Stalk Celery
1 Medium Apple
½-Inch Piece Gingerroot

1. Peel, cut, deseed, and/or chop the ingredients as needed.

2. Place a container under the juicer's spout.

3. Feed the ingredients one at a time, in the order listed, through the juicer.

4. Stir the juice and pour into glasses to serve.

Green Machine Juice Blend

SERVES 3-4

This juice is packed with all the vitamins and minerals you need for sustenance. Not only is it incredibly nutritious, it also has a unique flavor provided by radishes and their greens.

6 Red Radishes With Greens
3 Plum Tomatoes
2 Medium Beets
2 Small Carrots
2 Large Stalks Celery
2 Cups Packed Parsley Leaves

1. Peel, cut, deseed, and/or chop the ingredients as needed.

2. Place a container under the juicer's spout.

3. Feed the ingredients one at a time, in the order listed, through the juicer.

4. Stir the juice and pour into glasses to serve.

Parsley Power Gulp

SERVES 2

Often used as a garnish rather than an essential ingredient in recipes, parsley actually has a number of significant health benefits. It's an excellent source of folate, which helps to prevent certain cancers, and it has diuretic properties to flush excess water from the body. Parsley is also one of the best natural sources for vitamin C.

1 Bunch Parsley Leaves
2 Medium Carrots
2 Large Stalks Celery
1 Small Apple

Peel, cut, deseed, and/or chop the ingredients as needed.

Place a container under the juicer's spout.

Feed the ingredients one at a time, in the order listed, through the juicer.

Stir the juice and pour into glasses to serve.

Tomato Gazpacho Juice
SERVES 2

Though gazpacho is traditionally served as a cold soup, in this recipe it transforms into a tasty beverage. Tomatoes contain over nine thousand different phytonutrients, including vitamin C, copper, iron, potassium, and magnesium. They are also a good source of lycopene, which may help prevent cancer and improve mental health.

4 Plum Tomatoes
2 Large Stalks Celery
1 Seedless Cucumber
1 Medium Carrot
1 Small Red Bell Pepper
½ Bunch Parsley Leaves
1 Lime
1 Green Onion

1. Peel, cut, deseed, and/or chop the ingredients as needed.

2. Place a container under the juicer's spout.

3. Feed the ingredients one at a time, in the order listed, through the juicer.

4. Stir the juice and pour into glasses to serve.

Spinach Lime Juice
SERVES 2

If you are in the mood for something fresh and simple, this juice may be just what you need. No muss, no fuss—just delicious.

2 Bunches Spinach Leaves
1 Medium Green Apple
1 Lime

1. Peel, cut, deseed, and/or chop the ingredients as needed.

2. Place a container under the juicer's spout.

3. Feed the ingredients one at a time, in the order listed, through the juicer.

4. Stir the juice and pour into glasses to serve.

Fabulous Fennel Juice Blend
SERVES 2

Fennel is not a vegetable most people have on their shopping list. Though somewhat uncommon, fennel is an excellent source of nutrition. Loaded with calcium, potassium, phosphorus, and vitamin C, it is particularly beneficial for the digestive system.

2 Medium Fennel Bulbs
1 Small Stalk Celery
1 Small Carrot
1 Medium Apple

1. Peel, cut, deseed, and/or chop the ingredients as needed.

2. Place a container under the juicer's spout.

3. Feed the ingredients one at a time, in the order listed, through the juicer.

4. Stir the juice and pour into glasses to serve.

Spirulina Avocado Juice
SERVES 2

Though not your typical juice, this spirulina avocado blend is packed with essential nutrients. Avocados are an excellent source of heart-healthy fats as well as potassium, which helps regulate blood pressure. Spirulina, cultivated from algae, helps to boost thyroid function.

2 Small Apples
1 Seedless Cucumber
1 Ripe Avocado
1 Teaspoon Spirulina Powder

1. Peel, cut, deseed, and/or chop the ingredients as needed.

2. Place a container under the juicer's spout.

3. Feed the apples and cucumber through the juicer.

4. In a blender or food processor, blend the avocado until smooth.

5. Stir the pureed avocado and spirulina into the juice and pour into glasses to serve.

Refreshing Red Bell Pepper Carrot Juice
SERVES 2

Bell peppers are rich in vitamin C, which plays a significant role in eye and gum health. They also contain vitamin A, which is instrumental for healthy skin.

5 Medium Carrots
3 Medium Green Apples
1 Large Red Bell Pepper

1. Peel, cut, deseed, and/or chop the ingredients as needed.

2. Place a container under the juicer's spout.

3. Feed the ingredients one at a time, in the order listed, through the juicer.

4. Stir the juice and pour into glasses to serve.

Skinny Green Juice
SERVES 2

This skinny juice packs a powerful punch. Made with nutritious, low-calorie ingredients like celery and cucumber, this juice will provide your body with a variety of nutrients without exceeding your calorie goal.

2 Large Stalks Celery
1 Cup Romaine Lettuce
1 Cup Baby Spinach Leaves
1 Cup Kale Leaves
1 Small Cucumber
6 Sprigs Parsley, Dill, Or Cilantro
2 Tablespoons Freshly Squeezed Lime Juice

1. Peel, cut, deseed, and/or chop the ingredients as needed.

2. Place a container under the juicer's spout.

3. Feed the celery, romaine, spinach, kale, cucumber, and parsley, dill, or cilantro through the juicer.

4. Stir the lime juice into the juice and pour into glasses to serve.

Carrot Celery Cleanse

SERVES 2

Though carrots and celery are the stars of this recipe, the garlic is not to be forgotten. Garlic helps to regulate blood sugar and cholesterol levels while also providing antimicrobial, antibiotic, and anti-cancer properties.

4 Large Carrots
3 Large Stalks Celery
2 Large Kale Leaves
½ Bunch Spinach Leaves
1 Clove Garlic
1 Green Chili

1. Peel, cut, deseed, and/or chop the ingredients as needed.

2. Place a container under the juicer's spout.

3. Feed the ingredients one at a time, in the order listed, through the juicer.

4. Stir the juice and pour into glasses to serve.

Kick-Start Veggie Juice
SERVES 2

This juice recipe is full of nutritious vegetables to help you kick-start your day. In addition to the health benefits of these vegetables, you also get the crisp, peppery flavor of celery and the freshness of cilantro.

2 Large Stalks Celery
1 Large Carrot
½ Romaine Lettuce Heart
½ Medium Cucumber
3 Sprigs Cilantro

1. Peel, cut, deseed, and/or chop the ingredients as needed.

2. Place a container under the juicer's spout.

3. Feed the ingredients one at a time, in the order listed, through the juicer.

4. Stir the juice and pour into glasses to serve.

Protein Power Juice
SERVES 2

Add a little protein to your favorite juice blends by stirring in a tablespoon of hempseed Hempseeds are rich in dietary fiber and essential fatty acids. In fact, hempseeds are a more complete protein source than milk, meat, and eggs.

1 Bunch Kale Leaves
1 Small Head Broccoli
1 Large Stalk Celery
½ Bunch Collard Greens
1 Tablespoon Hempseed

1. Peel, cut, deseed, and/or chop the ingredients as needed.

2. Place a container under the juicer's spout.

3. Feed the first four ingredients one at a time, in the order listed, through the juicer.

4. Stir the hempseed into the juice and pour into glasses to serve.

Breakfast of Champions Juice

SERVES 2

Carrots are not only the most readily available vegetable, they are also incredibly rich in vitamins and minerals. In addition, carrots also contain beta-carotene and carotenoids, which help reduce the risk for cancer and cardiovascular disease.

6 Medium Carrots
2 Small Beets
2 Medium Apples
2 Cups Packed Baby Spinach Leaves
¼ Cup Mint Leaves

1. Peel, cut, deseed, and/or chop the ingredients as needed.

2. Place a container under the juicer's spout.

3. Feed the ingredients one at a time, in the order listed, through the juicer.

4. Stir the juice and pour into glasses to serve.

Green Garden Delight

SERVES 2

This recipe is loaded with healthy vegetables, including carrots, celery, bell pepper, and spinach. Spinach is known for its choline content. Choline is a B-complex vitamin that supports cognitive function. These benefits, combined with the nutrients in the other ingredients, create a juice that is perfectly delightful.

2 Cups Baby Spinach Leaves
1 Large Carrot
1 Large Stalk Celery
½ Medium Green Bell Pepper
½ Bunch Parsley
½ Bunch Cilantro

1. Peel, cut, deseed, and/or chop the ingredients as needed.

2. Place a container under the juicer's spout.

3. Feed the ingredients one at a time, in the order listed, through the juicer.

4. Stir the juice and pour into glasses to serve.

Cucumber Wake-Up Call

SERVES 2

Cucumbers are a good source of B vitamins, which help to regulate blood pressure. Combined with hearty kale, spinach, and the light sweetness of apple, this juice will give you something to wake up for.

2 Medium Cucumbers
2 Large Kale Leaves
1 Cup Baby Spinach Leaves
1 Medium Apple

1. Peel, cut, deseed, and/or chop the ingredients as needed.

2. Place a container under the juicer's spout.

3. Feed the ingredients one at a time, in the order listed, through the juicer.

4. Stir the juice and pour into glasses to serve.

Best Foot Forward Juice
SERVES 2

Parsnips are valued for their anti-cancer properties as well as their high levels of iron and calcium. Together with carrots, celery, and cucumber, they help this juice provide you with the nutrition needed to get your day off to a wonderful start.

2 Large Carrots
1 Large Stalk Celery
1 Medium Cucumber
1 Parsnip With Greens
½ Lemon

1. Peel, cut, deseed, and/or chop the ingredients as needed.

2. Place a container under the juicer's spout.

3. Feed the ingredients one at a time, in the order listed, through the juicer.

4. Stir the juice and pour into glasses to serve.

Pumpkin Pie Juice
SERVES 2

Rather than reaching for that extra slice of pumpkin pie, try this juice instead! Pumpkin is an excellent source of vitamins C and E, and it also has anti-inflammatory and blood-sugar stabilizing properties.

2 Cups Pumpkin
2 Medium Apples
1 Cup Cold Water
1 Teaspoon Pumpkin Pie Spice
1 Teaspoon Raw Honey

Peel, cut, deseed, and/or chop the ingredients as needed.

Place a container under the juicer's spout.

Feed the pumpkin and apples through the juicer.

Stir the water, pumpkin pie spice, and honey into the juice and pour into glasses to serve.

Liver Detox Tonic
SERVES 2

Ginger is highly valued for its detoxification properties. In this recipe, it marries perfectly with the nutrients found in kale and bok choy to create a delicious drink that's almost too good to be true.

1 Small Baby Bok Choy
3 Large Kale Leaves
1 Medium Apple
1 Small Lemon
½-Inch Piece Gingerroot

1. Peel, cut, deseed, and/or chop the ingredients as needed.

2. Place a container under the juicer's spout.

3. Feed the ingredients one at a time, in the order listed, through the juicer.

4. Stir the juice and pour into glasses to serve.

Summer Squash Supreme
SERVES 2

Summer squash is not a vegetable you often see in juicing recipes. It makes a wonderful addition, however, because it is low in calories but high in antioxidants that help repair damage caused by free radicals.

4 Cups Summer Squash
1 Large Apple
2 Cinnamon Sticks

1. Peel, cut, deseed, and/or chop the ingredients as needed.

2. Place a container under the juicer's spout.

3. Feed the squash and apple through the juicer.

4. Pour into glasses and serve with the cinnamon sticks.

Beet Berry Blast
SERVES 2

This juice recipe is the perfect combination of nutritious vegetables and fresh fruit flavor. Topped off with a handful of cilantro, this juice is both healthy and refreshing!

3 Medium Beets
2 Large Stalks Celery
1½ Cups Mixed Berries
1 Medium Apple
½ Bunch Cilantro Leaves

1. Peel, cut, deseed, and/or chop the ingredients as needed.

2. Place a container under the juicer's spout.

3. Feed the ingredients one at a time, in the order listed, through the juicer.

4. Stir the juice and pour into glasses to serve.

Minty Mojito Juice
SERVES 2

The fresh herbs in this juice combine beautifully with zesty lime. If you are craving that mojito flavor, but would rather go for something a little more nutritious, try this!

1 Medium Cucumber
½ Cup Packed Mint Leaves
½ Cup Packed Basil Leaves
1 Medium Apple
1 Lime

1. Peel, cut, deseed, and/or chop the ingredients as needed.

2. Place a container under the juicer's spout.

3. Feed the ingredients one at a time, in the order listed, through the juicer.

4. Stir the juice and pour into glasses to serve.

Cool Cilantro Coconut Juice
SERVES 3

This cool juice is just what you need on a hot summer day. Enjoy it while relaxing by the pool, or use it to rehydrate your body after a tough workout.

½ Bunch Cilantro
½ Lime
4 Cups Coconut Water

1. Peel, cut, deseed, and/or chop the ingredients as needed.

2. Place a container under the juicer's spout.

3. Feed the cilantro and lime through the juicer.

4. Stir the coconut water into the juice and pour into glasses to serve.

CHAPTER NINE
GREEN JUICES

"There's a major distinction between pasteurized juice and cold-pressed juice.... When juice is pasteurized, it's heated at a very high temperature, which protects it against bacteria and prolongs shelf life. However, this heating process also destroys live enzymes, minerals, and other beneficial nutrients. Cold pressing... extracts juice by crushing the fruits and vegetables... all without using heat."

Beautiful Beet Juice

SERVES 2

When you hear the word "beauty," beets may not be what come, to mind. Beet greens are, however, loaded with healthy vitamins and minerals that will rejuvenate your body and your appearance.

2 Cups Beet Greens
½ Small Cucumber
½ Small Head Green Cabbage
½ Bunch Parsley

1. Peel, cut, deseed, and/or chop the ingredients as needed.

2. Place a container under the juicer's spout.

3. Feed the ingredients one at a time, in the order listed, through the juicer.

4. Stir the juice and pour into glasses to serve.

Green Good Morning Juice

SERVES 2

This juice is loaded with leafy greens to help you start your day off right. Romaine lettuce is rich in vitamins C, A, and K, as well as minerals, including iron, potassium, magnesium, and manganese.

½ Bunch Spinach Leaves
2 Large Romaine Lettuce Leaves
2 Large Swiss Chard Leaves
2 Small Cucumbers
1 Small Apple
1-Inch Piece Gingerroot

1. Peel, cut, deseed, and/or chop the ingredients as needed.

2. Place a container under the juicer's spout.

3. Feed the ingredients one at a time, in the order listed, through the juicer.

4. Stir the juice and pour into glasses to serve.

Green Goodness Juice
SERVES 2

This juice is aptly named because it is, after all, full of green goodness. With ingredients like cabbage, cucumber, kale, and green bell pepper, this juice is nothing short of amazing.

1 Cup Carrots
1 Cup Green, Red, Or Savoy Cabbage
1 Small Cucumber
1 Small Green Bell Pepper
1 Large Kale Leaf
1 Small Bunch Cilantro

1. Peel, cut, deseed, and/or chop the ingredients as needed.

2. Place a container under the juicer's spout.

3. Feed the ingredients one at a time, in the order listed, through the juicer.

4. Stir the juice and pour into glasses to serve.

Glorious Green Juice

SERVES 2

As a low-calorie ingredient, celery is excellent in any green juice. Celery is also a good source of silicon, which helps strengthen bones and joints.

3 Large Red Chard Leaves
2 Large Kale Leaves
2 Large Stalks Celery
1 Cup Packed Baby Spinach Leaves
½ Small Head Broccoli
1 Medium Pear

1. Peel, cut, deseed, and/or chop the ingredients as needed.

2. Place a container under the juicer's spout.

3. Feed the ingredients one at a time, in the order listed, through the juicer.

4. Stir the juice and pour into glasses to serve.

Seven-Layer Green Juice
SERVES 2

Seven nutritious ingredients, one delicious beverage. The beauty of this green juice is that you can mix and match whatever vegetables you have on hand to create your own flavor combinations!

1 Cup Green Cabbage
1 Large Stalk Celery
1 Small Sweet Potato
½ Small Cucumber
½ Small Green Bell Pepper
½ Cup Fennel Bulb
1-Inch Piece Gingerroot

1. Peel, cut, deseed, and/or chop the ingredients as needed.

2. Place a container under the juicer's spout.

3. Feed the ingredients one at a time, in the order listed, through the juicer.

4. Stir the juice and pour into glasses to serve.

Dreamy Green Juice

SERVES 3

Packed with all the nutritious goodness of kale, zucchini, and broccoli, this juice is positively dreamy.

4 Large Curly Kale Leaves
3 Medium Apples
1 Medium Zucchini
1 Small Head Broccoli

1. Peel, cut, deseed, and/or chop the ingredients as needed.

2. Place a container under the juicer's spout.

3. Feed the ingredients one at a time, in the order listed, through the juicer.

4. Stir the juice and pour into glasses to serve.

Brilliant Brussels Juice
SERVES 2

Brussels sprouts have been linked to cancer prevention and they are also known to support body detoxification. These vegetables are also rich in vitamins and minerals. In fact, a single cup of Brussels sprouts contains your entire daily value of vitamins C and K.

12 Brussels Sprouts
4 Large Kale Leaves
1 Large Apple

1. Peel, cut, deseed, and/or chop the ingredients as needed.

2. Place a container under the juicer's spout.

3. Feed the ingredients one at a time, in the order listed, through the juicer.

4. Stir the juice and pour into glasses to serve.

Spicy Green Juice
SERVES 2

If you are looking for a juice that has a little kick, then look no further. In addition to its spicy flavor, ginger is also known for its detoxification benefits. This root has anti-inflammatory properties and it will help to support healthy digestion.

4 Large Swiss Chard Leaves
4 Large Collard Green Leaves
1 Small Head Green Cabbage
1-Inch Piece Gingerroot

1. Peel, cut, deseed, and/or chop the ingredients as needed.

2. Place a container under the juicer's spout.

3. Feed the ingredients one at a time, in the order listed, through the juicer.

4. Stir the juice and pour into glasses to serve.

Mango Tango Green Juice
SERVES 2

If eating vegetables is a chore, this juice will let you off the hook. You still get the nutritional benefits of vegetables like kale and spinach, but all you taste is the sweet flavor of mango.

4 Large Kale Leaves
3 Large Stalks Celery
1 Ripe Mango
1 Small Bunch Spinach Leaves

1. Peel, cut, deseed, and/or chop the ingredients as needed.

2. Place a container under the juicer's spout.

3. Feed the ingredients one at a time, in the order listed, through the juicer.

4. Stir the juice and pour into glasses to serve.

Easy Peasy Green Lemonade

SERVES 2

This scrumptious green juice combines the refreshing taste of lemonade with the many health benefits of melon, asparagus, and pear.

1 Small Honeydew Melon
1 Bunch Asparagus
1 Medium Pear
1 Lemon

1. Peel, cut, deseed, and/or chop the ingredients as needed.

2. Place a container under the juicer's spout.

3. Feed the ingredients one at a time, in the order listed, through the juicer.

4. Stir the juice and pour into glasses to serve.

Double Trouble Broccoli Juice
SERVES 2

Broccoli rabe is a cruciferous vegetable that resembles broccoli but doesn't form a large head. The leaves, buds, and stems are edible, and along with broccoli, all contain high levels of dietary fiber, iron, potassium, and vitamins C and E.

1 Small Head Broccoli
1 Bunch Broccoli Rabe
1 Large Apple
1 Clove Garlic

1. Peel, cut, deseed, and/or chop the ingredients as needed.

2. Place a container under the juicer's spout.

3. Feed the ingredients one at a time, in the order listed, through the juicer.

4. Stir the juice and pour into glasses to serve.

Tossed Salad Juice

SERVES 3

If you don't have time to sit down to eat a salad, this salad-inspired juice is just as good—or even better! With all of the ingredients you would find in a tossed salad, this refreshing beverage will satisfy your hunger and fill your body with healthy nutrients.

1 Romaine Lettuce Heart
6 Medium Carrots
3 Medium Stalks Celery
1 Medium Cucumber
1 Clove Garlic

1. Peel, cut, deseed, and/or chop the ingredients as needed.

2. Place a container under the juicer's spout.

3. Feed the ingredients one at a time, in the order listed, through the juicer.

4. Stir the juice and pour into glasses to serve.

Cool Cauliflower Juice
SERVES 3

Cauliflower is rich in phosphorus, potassium, manganese, and vitamin K. It is also a good source of glucosinolates, which help support your liver in its natural detoxification abilities.

12 Brussels Sprouts
1 Small Head Cauliflower
3 Radishes With Greens
1 Large Carrot
½ Small Head Green Cabbage

1. Peel, cut, deseed, and/or chop the ingredients as needed.

2. Place a container under the juicer's spout.

3. Feed the ingredients one at a time, in the order listed, through the juicer.

4. Stir the juice and pour into glasses to serve.

Merry Melon Dream Juice

SERVES 2

Fennel is known for its beneficial effects on the digestive system as well as its vitamin and mineral content. In this recipe, the rich flavors of fennel and asparagus are perfectly complemented by the light sweetness of cantaloupe.

4 Large Kale Leaves
½ Bunch Asparagus
½ Ripe Cantaloupe
½ Fennel Bulb

1. Peel, cut, deseed, and/or chop the ingredients as needed.

2. Place a container under the juicer's spout.

3. Feed the ingredients one at a time, in the order listed, through the juicer.

4. Stir the juice and pour into glasses to serve.

Sensibly Sweet Juice
SERVES 2

If you aren't a fan of overly sweetened juice, this pleasantly mild one may be the right choice for you. With only three ingredients, it is simple and simply delicious.

6 Large Stalks Celery
½ Head Romaine Lettuce
1 Large Apple

1. Peel, cut, deseed, and/or chop the ingredients as needed.

2. Place a container under the juicer's spout.

3. Feed the ingredients one at a time, in the order listed, through the juicer.

4. Stir the juice and pour into glasses to serve.

Refreshing Green Juice

SERVES 3

This recipe combines the crispness of bell pepper and cucumber with the fresh bite of cilantro to create an utterly refreshing juice.

6 Medium Carrots
2 Large Stalks Celery With Leaves
1 Bunch Cilantro
1 Medium Green Bell Pepper
1 Medium Cucumber
½ Bunch Spinach Leaves
1 Clove Garlic

1. Peel, cut, deseed, and/or chop the ingredients as needed.

2. Place a container under the juicer's spout.

3. Feed the ingredients one at a time, in the order listed, through the juicer.

4. Stir the juice and pour into glasses to serve.

Deeply Green Juice

SERVES 3

This recipe yields a nutritious juice with a beautiful deep green color. Most of this color can be attributed to kale, which has the highest vegetable source of vitamin K.

1 Bunch Curly Kale Leaves
1 Bunch Dandelion Greens
3 Sprigs Parsley
1 Large Apple
½ Medium Head Cabbage

1. Peel, cut, deseed, and/or chop the ingredients as needed.

2. Place a container under the juicer's spout.

3. Feed the ingredients one at a time, in the order listed, through the juicer.

4. Stir the juice and pour into glasses to serve.

Beets Me Blend
SERVES 3

If you have ever had beets, you may have been turned off by their dark purple color and strong odor. In this recipe, the beet flavor is disguised by the sweetness of apple juice and the fresh kick of ginger.

2 Medium Beets
1 Large Head Broccoli
1 Bunch Kale Leaves
½ Bunch Asparagus
1 Medium Apple
½-Inch Piece Gingerroot

1. Peel, cut, deseed, and/or chop the ingredients as needed.

2. Place a container under the juicer's spout.

3. Feed the ingredients one at a time, in the order listed, through the juicer.

4. Stir the juice and pour into glasses to serve.

Simply Sweet Green Juice

SERVES 3

Bok choy is a common ingredient in Asian cuisine, but in this recipe it provides both flavor and a variety of phytonutrients. Bok choy is an excellent source of fiber and antioxidants, which combine to provide anti-cancer and cholesterol-reducing benefits.

1 Head Baby Bok Choy
1 Small Head Broccoli
1 Medium Cucumber
½ Medium Zucchini
1 Kiwi
1 Medium Apple
1 Clove Garlic

1. Peel, cut, deseed, and/or chop the ingredients as needed.

2. Place a container under the juicer's spout.

3. Feed the ingredients one at a time, in the order listed, through the juicer.

4. Stir the juice and pour into glasses to serve.

Rocket Fuel Green Juice

SERVES 3

Blast off with this delectable, nutrient-packed green juice. Made with fresh greens such as arugula and kale, this juice has all the nutrients you need to start your day. Arugula, for example, is loaded with flavonoids, which help reduce cancer risk.

1 Bunch Arugula
½ Bunch Kale Leaves
6 Medium Carrots
2 Medium Apples
1 Red Chili Pepper
1 Clove Garlic

1. Peel, cut, deseed, and/or chop the ingredients as needed.

2. Place a container under the juicer's spout.

3. Feed the ingredients one at a time, in the order listed, through the juicer.

4. Stir the juice and pour into glasses to serve.

Get-Up-and-Go Juice
SERVES 2

This vitamin-packed energy juice is full of the nutrients you need to start your day off right. Lightly sweetened with apple juice and kiwis, this beverage is everything you could ever ask for in the morning.

4 Large Collard Green Leaves
2 Medium Apples
2 Ripe Kiwis
1 Small Head Broccoli
1 Clove Garlic

1. Peel, cut, deseed, and/or chop the ingredients as needed.

2. Place a container under the juicer's spout.

3. Feed the ingredients one at a time, in the order listed, through the juicer.

4. Stir the juice and pour into glasses to serve.

Sweet and Simple Green Juice

SERVES 2

You may be surprised to see dandelion greens as an ingredient in this recipe. Dandelion greens are actually a great source of vitamin K, which is essential for blood and bone health. These greens also support healthy liver and gallbladder function.

½ Bunch Spinach Leaves
½ Bunch Dandelion Greens
2 Large Carrots
1 Small Apple
1 Small Pear

1. Peel, cut, deseed, and/or chop the ingredients as needed.

2. Place a container under the juicer's spout.

3. Feed the ingredients one at a time, in the order listed, through the juicer.

4. Stir the juice and pour into glasses to serve.

Jolly Green Giant Juice

SERVES 3

This juice with gigantic flavor and nutrients will leave you feeling lean and mean. Packed with vitamin-loaded ingredients like broccoli and romaine lettuce, this juice is more than just a beverage—it is fuel for your body.

4 Large Stalks Celery
2 Medium Heads Broccoli
2 Medium Apples
½ Head Romaine Lettuce
½ Lemon

1. Peel, cut, deseed, and/or chop the ingredients as needed.

2. Place a container under the juicer's spout.

3. Feed the ingredients one at a time, in the order listed, through the juicer.

4. Stir the juice and pour into glasses to serve.

Lean, Mean Green Juice

SERVES 2

Leafy greens like kale and Swiss chard are packed with vitamin K, calcium, and iron. They are also some of the most nutrient-dense vegetables in existence, which means you get all the benefits for very few calories!

4 Large Curly Kale Leaves
4 Large Swiss Chard Leaves
2 Large Carrots
½ Small Head Broccoli
1 Medium Apple

1. Peel, cut, deseed, and/or chop the ingredients as needed.

2. Place a container under the juicer's spout.

3. Feed the ingredients one at a time, in the order listed, through the juicer.

4. Stir the juice and pour into glasses to serve.

Green Goddess Juice

SERVES 2

Feel like a goddess (or god!) after drinking this delightful green juice. Full of healthy vitamins and minerals, it will leave you feeling utterly refreshed.

4 Large Kale Leaves
1 Cup Pineapple
½ Bunch Spinach Leaves
1 Medium Apple

1. Peel, cut, deseed, and/or chop the ingredients as needed.

2. Place a container under the juicer's spout.

3. Feed the ingredients one at a time, in the order listed, through the juicer.

4. Stir the juice and pour into glasses to serve.

CONCLUSION

If it has become a challenge to fit your daily servings of fruit and vegetables into your routine, juicing is the perfect solution. You can get an entire salad's worth of fresh produce into a single glass of sip-able juice.

Not only is juicing quick and easy, but it is also good for you! By replacing unhealthy meals with fresh-pressed juices that are loaded with vitamins and minerals, you can significantly improve your overall health. Once you stop loading down your body with toxins and additives, your body will begin to efficiently process nutrients, resulting in healthier hair, skin, nails, and organs. Additionally, you are also likely to experience improved digestion, and if it is your goal, healthy and sustainable weight loss. Juicing is a wonderful option for the whole family, so try out some of the delicious recipes in this book together and improve your health today.

Printed by Libri Plureos GmbH in Hamburg, Germany